Autumn Notes

A Collection of Poems

by

Elizabeth Patton

Downtown Books & Coffee
Auburn, NY

Publication Credits
For Poems Appearing in Autumn Notes:

"In Concert," *Eleven*
"Women in Houses," *Art Times*
"Widow's Watch," *Potato Eyes*
"Inside Information," *Bloodroot*
"Silent Legacy," *The Peacock's Feet*
"Retirement," *Emerson of Harvard*

Copyright © 2012 by Elizabeth Patton

All rights reserved.

Published in the United States by
Downtown Books Publishing
66 Genesee Street
Auburn, NY 13021
www.downtownbooksandcoffee.com

Cover Design: Ryan Zygarowicz-Bartlett
Cover Photo: Elizabeth Patton
Author Photo: Marcus Devoe

Contents

In Concert
1

Sharing Lives at the Drugstore
2

Chance Encounter
3

The Wildebeest
4

Time Goes By
5

Seeing You After
6

The Old Vaudeville Couple
7

Women in Houses
8

Gertrude Thinks About the Latest Picture
9

Cape Cod Evening, 1939
10

I Was Wondering, Pierre,
11

Sketching the Evening Landscape
13

Inventing a History of Preston Hollow, 12469
14

Remembering Vercingetorix
16

A Word to the Man Who Thought He Was but Wasn't
17

Silent Legacy
19

Widow's Watch
20

New Year's Eve
21

Saying Goodbye to Tom
22

Ninth Inning
24

Canning Tomatoes After
25

Setting the Stage
26

Inside Information
27

Retirement: Just a Literary Term
28

For the Woman With Too Many Books
29

The Collector
30

Retirement
32

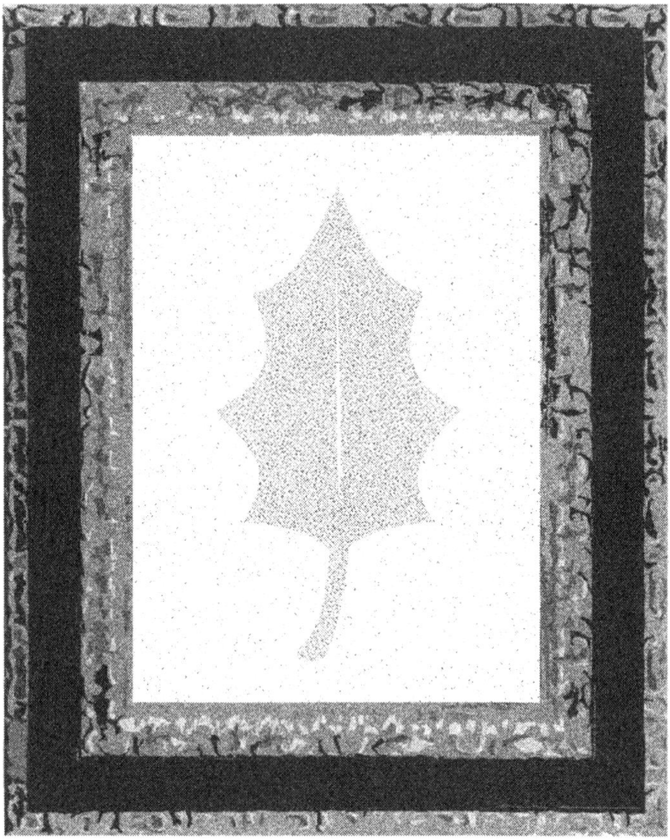

In Concert

Once in the middle of a concert

When Bach alone with the instrument

Moved

He handed her his program

And she read I love you

In the velvet gloom

And listened

Knowing that she would keep

It and take it out

To read again

When this moment passed

And he had forgotten

That he could ever do

Anything like that.

Sharing Lives at the Drugstore

She gave me the New York Times.
She asked me about gardening.
I told her I was transplanting
hydrangeas. She seemed pleased
that I was making progress.

I asked her how long she
would be working. "I'm off
3:30." "And then what?"
I asked. "My mother is here
from France, and my boyfriend
and I will spend time with her."

I told her that I'd been to France twice
and loved Provence. "You should go back.
My parents live in Marseille,
and you could stay with them."

What a pretty girl, I thought,
but the Becky on her nametag
didn't fit. What about Claudine
or Collete or Scheherazade? I
always like a good story.
Maybe she'll continue
her story another day.

Chance Encounter

Crossing the street

from a theater performance

I saw him and remembered

him from London theaters.

he saw me and we gave those

little squeals of recognition,

that sounded like reunited children

on the playground.

After an embrace, we

parted, both thinking

who was that person? We knew each other

but the names had fallen

into a toiling abyss.

It's that time of life when

faces somehow hang onto

the edges of memory,

and the names slip away.

The Wildebeest

I spend my life running.
looking for zebras to give me stripes.
knowing that jackals are not fooled.
Sometimes I am not quick enough,
and I bleed, feeling the mouths on me.

Then I see the zebras galloping on,
their dusty forms stamped on stereopticon
plates my grandmother dropped into slots
and adjusted. *AND HERE ARE THE PLAINS
OF THE SERENGETI*, she would announce, never
thinking that my flesh might be chewed.

Time Goes By

Saturday night
between 8:30
and 9, I sit
cuppa in hand
and visit Jean
and Lionel.

Even away from home,
I try to see them.
Once on a trip
to visit friends,
I discovered Jean
and Lionel
in another house.

Our visit did not
cancel our time
in London, the four
of us sitting
and drinking tea
and visiting Jean
and Lionel.

As time went by,
four became one.
Jean and Lionel
understood, their
lives going on
and starting over,
drinking tea with me
and never growing old.

Seeing You After

All I had heard about you;
where you went, what you did,
and now you sit somewhere
listening as I listen.
I know you're in the room.
A friend has already told me
that you came with her.
Someone I'd like, she said.

When you come to me
during intermission,
You come without her.
I want to ask about the rabbit,
something I couldn't have
in the settlement. I wonder
if you've changed your mind.
I've been collecting others,
and I really would like him
on my hearth, where we set him
so that he could watch
over us and smile, you said.

Instead, I tell you that I have
a poem coming out and that I
am getting old. You agree at last
to be old, too. I never see her.

The Old Vaudeville Couple

He didn't want to leave me
in Altoona, so he put me
in his act. I could sing
and dance a little, and he said
I was swell – a real trooper.
(He was like that.) So we
took to the boards.

He took care of business
and told me where we were
going next. I just packed
the trunk. He signed the checks
and we sang and danced:
Another city, another stage,
another audience,
another boarding house,
the same routine.

Now he dances slower.
He forgets the words.
I dance faster and belt
out the songs. Tonight
they played us off the stage.
I hold his hand
as we go to our dressing room.

The time will come
to take him home,
but I don't know where home is.

Women in Houses

When the sun floods

    my window

I think of

    Vermeer's women

    smiling over

    pearls and wine

    letters and lace

but I see myself

    outside

    in The Little Street

a woman over

    a barrel

some children on

    the pavement

Gertrude Thinks About the Latest Picture (Ninety Sessions and Then a Quick Fix)

Just when Pablo seemed
to be ready to clean
his brushes, he painted

out the face,
propped the canvas
against the wall,

and took off
for the Pyrenees.
Back in Paris, he

painted in that head
no one else liked –
my brother, my friends

could not understand
why I liked it. I
once told Pablo that

a burglar could break
in and take his painting
and my manuscripts

and have all the good
stuff, and we laughed,
I with my bass, Pablo

hitting the high notes.
To think that Spaniard used
my head to ease into Africa.

Cape Cod Evening, 1939
Edward Hopper

I didn't go to church
        today. I guess I've
        lost interest in God.
        since our son died.

My wife went today;
        she's a believer.
        Sunday for her
        is the same except
        for the empty chair
        at the table.

We had plans for our son:
        we wanted him
        to join me at the
        auto shop. He could
        have taken over
        the house when we
        retired. His future
        was secure, we thought.

We took his dog. I'm
        trying to get him
        to accept us and
        the old house, but
        he looks away, still
        waiting for our son.

I look at him and wonder
        when he will know
        what we know.

I Was Wondering, Pierre,

Why you painted all those women

behind tables (over ninety pictures

of tables)

You covered the women with orange

and purple and red and let them

stare around

Maybe you caught your wife

trying to get up enough energy

to finish clearing the dishes

or your daughter sitting at the table

until she could get down those

anchovies (they don't grow on trees)

or your mother-in-law left in a café when

you excused yourself to go to the men's

room but really went home to get out

the ochre and viridian and cerulean

and paint some more women without feet

Of course, that's it. You, Pierre Bonnard,

could paint faces, hands, tables, chairs,

windows, but you couldn't paint feet.

Sketching the Evening Landscape

On my left a dark figure
waits for me to pass.
I pass, and he follows
on a skateboard.

I pull into my driveway
and wait, watching
his shadow, hardly
hearing the wheels.

Beyond the pines
he appears, disappears,
reappears, a dab
of Payne's grey.

Inventing a History of Preston Hollow 12469

The men promised
the women they
would cut trees,
clear fields, build
houses close together.

The women packed china,
linens, furniture,
paintings and stuffed
old boots with roses,
lilacs, irises, lilies,
and peonies. They knew
how to make homes
and they did.

They talked about
the weather, the stars,
and the moon
and watched the
sun set over the water.
Once they locked doors
and lit candles,
the nights were
never frightening.

They kept their customs,
wrote in journals,
and sent letters
back East. They told
of births and deaths
and departures,
and they held on.

Autumn Notes

Driving down 145,
I want to stop,
but never do,
always passing by,
hurrying on. The houses
seemed abandoned,
but there are inviting signs:
Books, Antiques,
Fresh Eggs. I should
stop one day and call out:

"Is anyone there?"
From the cemetery
I hear the murmur
of lost voices: "Come
back. We're still here.
We held on, close together."

Remembering Vercingetorix

In September Caesar once again
crossed into Gaul. It always seemed warm,
the heat in the classroom and the heat
from the burning fields the Helvetians set.
I felt sorry for them – all that work
and then having to torch the crops.

We kept moving, but the scenes are hazy now.
Mostly I remember impedimenta.
The Romans seemed to have it in abundance
or should I say them? Anyway, they
were loaded down, and the orders kept coming,
and they kept moving.

We were moving faster and faster
through the pages. The year was nearly over,
and we'd fought long enough.
But then there was Vercingetorix,
who had to be subdued.
By then I wanted some variety. I wanted
Caesar to lose. Suppose Vercingetorix
had written his memoirs?

I like to think that some descendant
was part of the group that startled
the geese and kept on going.

A Word to the Man Who Thought He Was but Wasn't

You made the papers,
holding up the picture
of a boy stolen years ago
on Long Island. Did
you really think you
were that boy? Did
you imagine that
your parents took off
after chores to drive
to Long Island and come
back with a rosy-cheeked
boy? Of course, you
weren't that boy,
but you kept saying
you believed you were
until DNA put a stop
to the newspaper articles.

There are misplaced
children all over. You
should know that.
I knew early on
that I was in the wrong
house, the wrong century.
I thought I had lived
before in England,
a much-loved daughter
of parents who read novels
and dressed for dinner.

At the Armistice
my father looked
around the table
and said, "That's that.

What can you do?
Life goes on." Afterwards
thinking of my two
brothers lost in the Argonne,
we sat quietly
by the fire, drank tea,
took a walk with the dogs,
and my mother
mentioned going
into London sometime
for books and theatre.

Those peaceful fantasies
helped me withstand
prolonged battles. You
just made the mistake
of telling people. The
trick is to pretend
and keep quiet,
your secret safe
as a smile, knowing
that you belong somewhere.

Silent Legacy

The land is still there

the wind blowing

      through the pecan trees

where once a house stood

      sheltered in the grove

the barn and crib leaving no signs

fences falling in on themselves

water following its own mystery

In the sand I found a few shards

of ironstone from our table

So little to mark the generations

      of our scattered family

Widows' Watch

After my neighbor died, his wife,
fearing the dark, turned on lights
all over the house—even
during the day. "I never lived
alone," she told me, "until now."
She imagined a man in her bedroom
closet, a vagrant in the basement,
a weirdo in the pantry. At night
she could hear them wandering
in the hall, turning off lights,
looking everywhere for her.

When my husband died, I left
our bedroom, moving downstairs
to save heat. In the new bed
My body kept wanting to point
north again. I slept adrift,
floating until I could touch
bottom and wade out every morning
into familiar territory.
At night I think of us steering
small boats: one without lights,
the other without a compass.

New Year's Eve
(And then there was one)

Year after year we celebrated
the end of the year,
the four of us: a fire, drinks,
dinner, and then champagne.

We never seemed to change.
Time passed with birthdays,
anniversaries, dinners,
and trips. The years went by.

But this year the table
is empty, the stove is cold,
and the four flutes are hanging
upside down under the upper
shelf of the cabinet. I look
at them and wonder if I'll
ever taste champagne again.

Saying Goodbye to Tom

A month ago we met, two wives,

our husbands, waiting for chemo,

talked of Ireland. I pushed

my husband's wheelchair.

Tom walked with energy, smiling

and joking. "He eats like a horse,"

his wife said. As the appointments

went by, Tom used a cane, then

a wheelchair. We always waved.

The last day Tom, his wife,

and his sons met the doctor

and the nurse practitioner

in a private room. As my husband

received chemo, we watched the door.

Soon she ran out crying, then

returned, then came out and walked

into a nurse's arms. The sons

came with Tom. As he passed us,

I waved, and he blew me a kiss.

Ninth Inning

He watches the hands
inching slowly toward
three o'clock. Once
again he asks
when the Yankees play.

Seven o'clock, I say,
but he can't understand
the concept of time.
Now? Now? He asks.
Not now. Seven o'clock.

Watching the clock
and waiting, he's now
in his last inning,
the Yankees holding him
to the time he has left.

Canning Tomatoes After

he died, I thought about
the planting, the staking,
the ripening, the gathering.
We were a team.

He would fill pans
with water, lift
the canner to the stove,
and turn on the gas.
I would drop the tomatoes
into boiling water and remove
the skins. He would empty
the pans into the composter,
and then wash them.

Filling jars, fishing out lids
and rings from the boiling
water, I would put them
in the rack. He would
tighten the rings. Fifteen
minutes to boil, and he would
lift the rack to the counter.

I always reminded him
that Del Monte did a good
job with tomatoes, and he
would say, "But they
don't have our Romas."

Setting the Stage

"I want a gourmet death, a BMW kind of death, a death with style and taste, like a Fine Bordeaux." – Richard Patton

I am thinking of a quiet, easeful death.

I will settle in for the night:

sitting in bed, reading a Trollope novel.

I'll pause to sip some Earl Grey.

Maybe one more chocolate covered cherry

before I turn off the light.

In a quiet moment the book will

snap shut, and I will hear

the last few words

of "There'll Always Be an England."

Inside Information

She wanted to be Peggy Lee
dressed in a black dress
draped on a totem pole:
a face carved from ice
and a voice that pulled
men from the masts of ships.
But she knew
that she could only
turn up the records
and dance barefoot on the rug
when they were gone.

Retirement: Just a Literary Term

I remember telling them not to use

Stereotypes in their stories.

When I mentioned the retired

English teacher, they easily

Filled in the blanks.

They could see her:

> Horned-rimmed glasses
>
> Hair in bun
>
> Sensible shoes
>
> Head in book
>
> Two cats
>
> Seven African violets

They could see her.

Now when they recognize me

Far from the classroom,

They tell me I haven't changed,

And they never wonder why

It's not a compliment.

For the Woman With Too Many Books

Her library, shelved,
stacked, scattered,
speaks to her: "Let me
tell you a story, you
need another trip,
try a new plant this year,
read a poem slowly,
solve another mystery."

She can't resist
the covers, the bios.
She keeps buying
even if the sale
is on the last day.
There are always
books for her.
She keeps reading
and listening.
Sometimes she can't
hear them and puts
them away as gifts.

She can't move away
and leave her books.
How could she
choose her favorites?
She could hear
them calling: "Take me!"

The Collector

I look over the fabrics
folded neatly in chests,
yards and yards of cloth
mated with new patterns.
I had plans.

I cannot remember
the provenance of the cloth.
Where did I buy it?
Why did I buy it?
I did buy it though
and stored it as I moved
from house to house,
state to state.
I had plans.

Even in foreign markets,
I collected cloth,
saving it for special
occasions which I
never attended.
I had dreams.

Sometimes I look
over the proposed
dresses, gowns, and skirts
and see myself preening
at the mirror, listening
to compliments.
Other times I see
fabric turned into gifts:
aprons, napkins,
pot holders and hear
recipients admiring
my work. "You made these?

Thank you so much."

There is something
in a woman that drives
her to plan and dream
and hold onto projects
until at last she knows
to let go and admit defeat.
I raise the white flag
and surrender, knowing
that an army of women
have served with me.

Retirement

This is a time to hold
onto a quiet life in my last
house, built generations ago
when workmen gathered stones
for foundations and fireplaces.

This is a place to comfort me:
shelves of books to read
or reread if I have time left;
above the books, teapots
lined up for inspection, all
brown and common enough
for farm tables and early mornings;
on cupboard shelves, family ironstone
that went to the West by wagon
and returned to the East by plane.

I sit, waiting for words that flutter
and disappear if I don't pin them
to paper. At the end, someone may say,
"She was the teacher who taught me to write."

Elizabeth Patton lives and writes in the Finger Lakes region of Central New York. Her work is widely published in literary and professional journals. She reads her poetry frequently at libraries, museums, bookstores and other venues. She is an active member of area writing groups, and her first chapbook, Late Harvest, was published by Pudding House Press in 2009.

Made in the USA
Charleston, SC
22 December 2012